COLORING
FOR CONTEMPLATION

COLORING
FOR CONTEMPLATION

Amber Hatch with Illustrations by Alex Ogg

WATKINS

Sharing Wisdom Since
1893

This edition first published in the USA and Canada 2015 by
Watkins, an imprint of Watkins Media Limited
19 Cecil Court, London WC2N 4EZ

enquiries@watkinspublishing.co.uk

Design and typography copyright © Watkins Media Limited 2015
Text copyright © Amber Hatch 2015
Illustrations copyright © Alex Ogg 2015

3 5 7 9 10 8 6 4 2

Designed by Clare Thorpe

Printed and bound in the United States of America

A CIP record for this book is available from the British Library

ISBN: 978-1-78028-925-0

www.watkinspublishing.com

CONTENTS

ACKNOWLEDGEMENTS

We'd like to thank our agent, Jane, of Graham Maw Christie, who helped seed the idea for this book. Thank you also to Jo Lal and her team at Watkins, who made working on this book an absolute pleasure.

Thanks to Eve and Jamie for looking after us in Devon!

We are both very grateful to our Samatha meditation teachers for sharing their wisdom so generously.

Alex—Thanks to Isabel, Garry and Fern for providing calm spaces where I could draw. I also want to thank my mum, Sarah, for nurturing a love of drawing from the beginning.

INTRODUCTION

Pick up your pens and pencils, and let's begin our journey ...

We have collected together a selection of our favorite sayings and teachings from around the world, and it is these insights that have inspired the images in this book.

We've called our book *Coloring for Contemplation*. By "contemplation," we mean slowing down and taking some time to notice what's around us, and exploring ideas—not in the sense of overthinking them, but rather sensing and playing with them. Contemplation also helps us consider how we can *be* in the world, which we do when we bring more awareness, or "mindfulness," to our thoughts.

By giving yourself the time and space—and permission—to color, you make room for contemplation in a busy world. And, as you complete each picture, you will also create a beautiful record of both your handiwork and your inner journey.

Everyone knows how to color, so there's no pressure or expectation. Even if you only have time for a minute or two in your day, you'll find that you access an oasis of calm while the pencil is in your hand.

SO WHAT IS MINDFULNESS?

The concept of mindfulness has its roots in Buddhist teachings, but it is not just an ancient religious custom.

Mindfulness is the quality of mind when you have brought your attention right into the present moment. When you are mindful, you are experiencing life as it is actually happening. You are not being pulled into the future or going over events from the past. Nor do you tell yourself stories about yourself or your experiences.

As mindfulness deepens, your sense of a separate self diminishes, allowing you to feel more connected to the world around you. Everybody can experience mindfulness. You may recognize this sensation at special moments, such as gazing at a beautiful sunset. But actually mindfulness can occur at any time: when going about your daily tasks or when doing an activity such as coloring.

CULTIVATING MINDFULNESS

The interesting thing about mindfulness is that it is not just a pleasant state that sometimes graces us; we can actually *cultivate* it. All we have to do is pay attention to what's happening in the present moment: in our body, in our mind and in our surroundings. We can "practice mindfulness" by bringing our attention to the present moment, again and again. Soon, the process becomes a mental habit, and mindfulness arises more easily and more often.

However, despite our best intentions, sometimes it is difficult to remember to be mindful, so we can help things along by setting aside specific times to practice. Some people do this by sitting quietly for a few minutes each day in formal meditation. Another way is to "attach" a mindfulness practice to a particular activity. For example, you could try to be mindful whenever you wash the dishes or when eating.

This book can also provide an opportunity for cultivating mindfulness. You can make a commitment to practice mindfulness whenever you are coloring. Then, whenever you pick up your pencil, you will be reminded to bring your attention back to the present moment. I'll talk more about the specifics of this in a moment.

WHY BE MINDFUL?
Recent Western scientific studies have shown that mindfulness practices have a measurable effect on wellbeing and happiness. This means that everybody can benefit from more mindfulness.

When we bring more awareness to our lives, we experience everything more fully. This means that all our senses are heightened: food tastes more flavorsome, smells sharper, colors brighter. When we are mindful we can watch where our thoughts are going, rather than be swept along with them. We are also more aware of our feelings, whether we feel joy, sadness, contentedness, or anger. And, when we are being mindful, it's easier to choose whether or not to act on those feelings.

Mindfulness helps us to be more real when we interact with our families, friends and colleagues. Being present helps us to see them, and their needs, as they really are, in that moment. It helps us listen carefully to what they are saying, and to reply thoughtfully. When we have our attention on the present moment, we can respond to it more fully. Without so many distracting thoughts, there is more space for other positive qualities to arise, such as joy, patience, compassion and wisdom.

In short, mindfulness helps us to be more alive.

COLORING AS A MEDITATION

As a simple activity, coloring lends itself well to contemplation. It does not require you to make too many decisions. Once you have chosen which color you wish to use, and which space to fill, you can just follow the lines. The soothing nature of the activity is relaxing and can help you to calm down, and eventually—even without any intention on your part—your thoughts become less hurried.

If you like, you can aid this process by increasing your mindfulness as you color. Each time you notice that your thoughts have wandered away from the task, you can note where they are and then gently bring your attention back to the pen or pencil in your hand. Although this instruction is very simple, it can be difficult to follow. At first it can feel like an effort—you'll be amazed at how active your mind really is. You may even find that several minutes go by before you realize you have lost awareness. Keeping the mind on task is rather like trying to keep a kitten in a basket: it keeps on climbing out. Remember to smile at its antics as you gently put it back.

If you keep bringing your mind back to the coloring in front of you, your thoughts will eventually settle down, and you will find that you can reach an even deeper level of calm and awareness.

HOW TO USE THIS BOOK

You will find 30 sets of quotations and images in this book. We have chosen teachings that aid contemplation and arranged them into the following sections:

MINDFULNESS

INSIGHT

INSPIRATION

We have arranged them in this order so that you can let the teachings take you on a journey. The first section encourages you to slow down, breathe and be present. The mindfulness you cultivate will help make space to grow other positive qualities. The next section helps you to find wonder all around, and experience the joy that this brings. In the last section, we chose the words that have inspired us to try to make a difference in the world—however small. We hope that these teachings inspire you too.

The illustrations play with the quotations: sometimes the images try to represent the words, in other cases the quotations give an extra layer of meaning to the image. We've found that using art to illustrate the teachings is a helpful way to explore their ideas because as we try to represent them visually, they become more than just words on a page. We start to understand them on a different sensory level.

Now, we invite you to join us in this exploration. Working on these images, you can help to create them fully. Your marks will add a new layer of interpretation to the ideas and you will find a deeper understanding of the texts. As you work, consider how your marks and colors change the image—which areas do they emphasize, which do they subdue? How does this new, colorful image interact with the text?

Art is also a way of expressing ourselves. Through interpreting the texts and images with colors, you give personal meaning to them. You are creating something that also, in part, represents your own inner development.

THE JOURNEY

We have talked about these pictures and words taking you on a journey, and you might choose to work on these images in the order that they appear. However, journeys of this kind are rarely linear and it is perfectly fine to "dip in" to the book wherever you please. Look for the images and texts that really resonate with you. When something strikes a chord with you, or reminds you of something particular in your own life, then it is a sign that this teaching is especially relevant to you right now. Trust in that inner knowledge: it will help you make the most of the ideas.

It's also worth looking out for ideas that perhaps jar with you, or seem flat, and explore why, because there can be a lot of learning here too. Or, perhaps, look for connections between the images and words across the sections, and explore which ideas lead to what. You may find surprising similarities between teachers from very different backgrounds and eras. Drawing your own connections between the texts is another way to interpret them and to make them more meaningful for you.

HOW TO USE THE GUIDED MEDITATIONS

You will find a guided meditation towards the end of each section. Each one expands on the theme of that section, but it's up to you how you use them. The first meditation, "on coloring," is best practiced while you work on a picture while the other two, "on a pencil" and "loving-kindness," are more suitable for practicing during a resting period. Or you might prefer to read all the meditations in advance of coloring and dip in to the ideas every now and again as you work.

REFLECTING ON YOUR WORK

At the end of each section, you will also find some pages titled "Reflections." These consist of a series of questions and some other ideas designed to help you expand on the theme. You may like to consider them after you have worked through the whole section or more regularly, perhaps after you have worked on a picture. Some of the ideas help you to look inwards while others suggest practical actions to explore the theme in your daily life.

If you wish to use this book as a journey guide, then consider writing in a journal alongside your coloring, so that you can note down your observations in more detail. The questions and suggestions in "Reflections" can act as a starting point for these jottings. You could keep a record of things you notice as you color and contemplate, or jot down more general ideas inspired by your reading and coloring. You'll find a specific suggestion for how to use your journal in each section.

At the end of "Reflections" there is also a blank page for you to use as you please—perhaps for notes or to draw your own pictures. A teaching may inspire you to create your own image or you might like to practice coloring techniques or test color combinations, which you could develop later.

Alternatively, you could use this space to create your own meditation—you could write it down, or even draw it.

TECHNIQUE

There are no rules when it comes to coloring, which can be both simple and subtle. But, if you would like to explore some new creative techniques, the following suggestions will give you some ideas.

- Not all pencils are created equal. Use high-quality colored pencils that mark the page easily and give a range of opacities according to subtle pressure differences.

- Choose to color the pictures in realistic colors, or use an abstract color scheme to bring emphasis to certain areas.

- You can color whole areas in block colors across the lines.

- Try watercolor pencils for a very intense color—but watch out for smudging!

- You can add variety and complexity by alternating colors within a group of spaces.

- You can use two colors in one space, either by blending them together gradually or creating a stark contrast.

- The narrow nibs of fineliner pens are ideal for outlines if you want to add extra detail to the pictures.

- Try felt-tip pens for vibrant, solid colors. Watch out for going over the same area too often as this can lead to darker patches or even impair the surface of the paper.

- Use fine-liners to "color in" with a pattern: hatching, ribbing, or dots for example. You can use them like this in conjunction with pencil crayons.

- Don't use colors: you can try finishing the picture with black, white, and gray.

TAKE A BREAK

Any type of handiwork can cause strain on your hand and wrist, so it's important to take regular breaks. Coloring can be particularly tricky as the action is very repetitive. Always stop if you feel discomfort and take regular breaks—at least every 15 to 20 minutes—even if you feel fine. Use this time as an opportunity to relax and observe your breath.

MINDFULNESS

When we bring our attention to the present moment, we find ourselves more open to experience, more connected, and able to live more fully.

The words in this section speak of the joy of finding the present moment to encourage, guide, and inspire us. Some of them remind us to slow down and take time to appreciate what's around us. Others point out that the present moment can be found anywhere— even in the most mundane actions of daily life.

Others help us to see how important it is for us to take responsibility for our own minds, and yet have patience with ourselves as we try to do that. If we want to be awake, it's up to us to pay attention— no one else can do that for us.

"Meditation is really very simple ... Like that dawn
that came up this morning, it comes silently,
and makes a golden path in the very stillness,
which was at the beginning, which is now,
and which will be always there."

JIDDU KRISHNAMURTI
SPIRITUAL TEACHER

(1895–1986)

"Rest is not idleness, and to lie sometimes on the grass under trees on a summer's day, listening to the murmur of the water, or watching the clouds float across the sky, is by no means a waste of time."

JOHN LUBBOCK
ENGLISH PHILANTHROPIST

(1834–1913)

"Do you have the patience to wait until your mud settles and the water is clear?"

LAO TZU
CHINESE PHILOSOPHER AND POET
(c. 6TH CENTURY BCE)

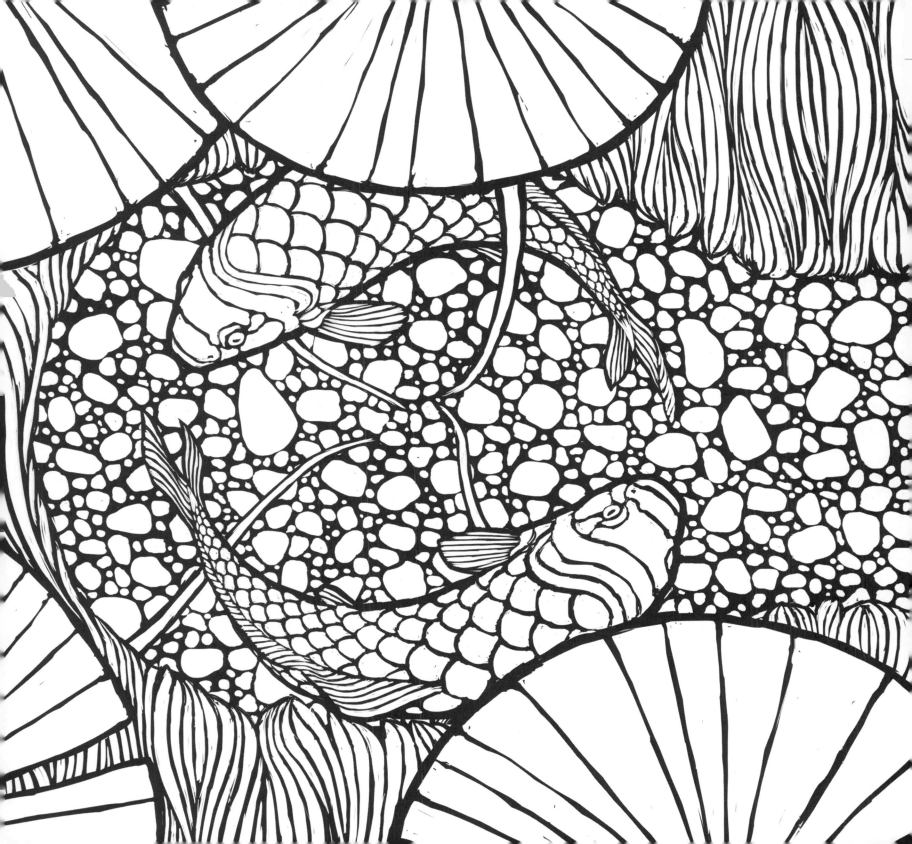

"O snail
Climb Mount Fuji,
But slowly, slowly!"

KOBAYASHI ISSA
JAPANESE HAIKU POET

(1763–1828)

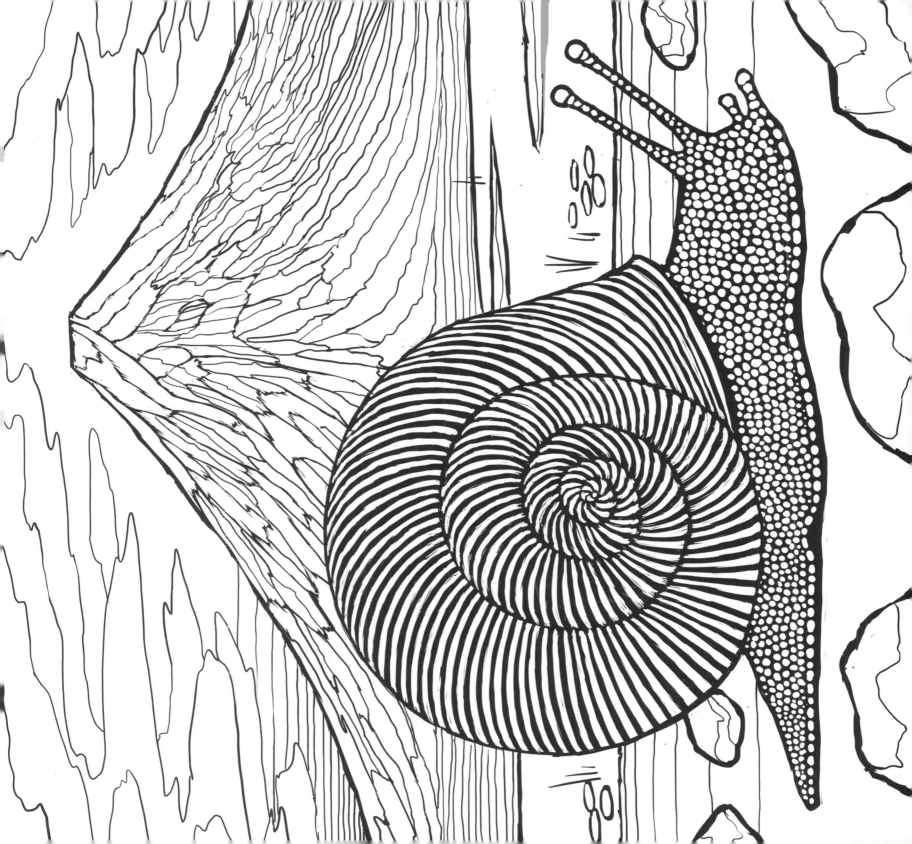

"Walk as if you are kissing the earth with your feet."

THICH NHAT HANH
VIETNAMESE ZEN MASTER AND PEACE ACTIVIST
(B. 1926)

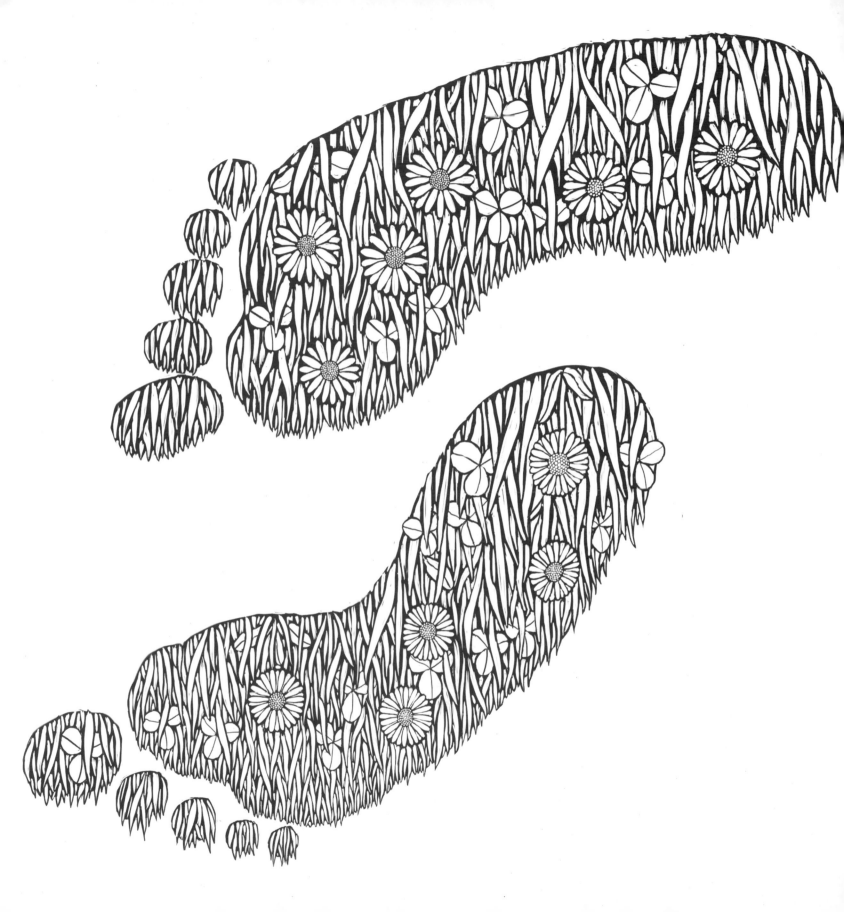

"Look inward.
Don't let the true nature of anything elude you.
Before long, all existing things will be transformed,
to rise like smoke (assuming all things become one),
or be dispersed in fragments."

MARCUS AURELIUS
ROMAN EMPEROR AND STOIC PHILOSOPHER

(121–180 CE)

"... if there is a state where the soul can find a resting-place secure enough to establish itself and concentrate its entire being there, with no need to remember the past or reach into the future ... with no sign of the passing of time, and no other feeling ... than the simple feeling of existence, a feeling that fills our soul entirely, as long as this state lasts, we can call ourselves happy ..."

JEAN-JACQUES ROUSSEAU
SWISS PHILOSOPHER, WRITER AND COMPOSER

(1712–1778)

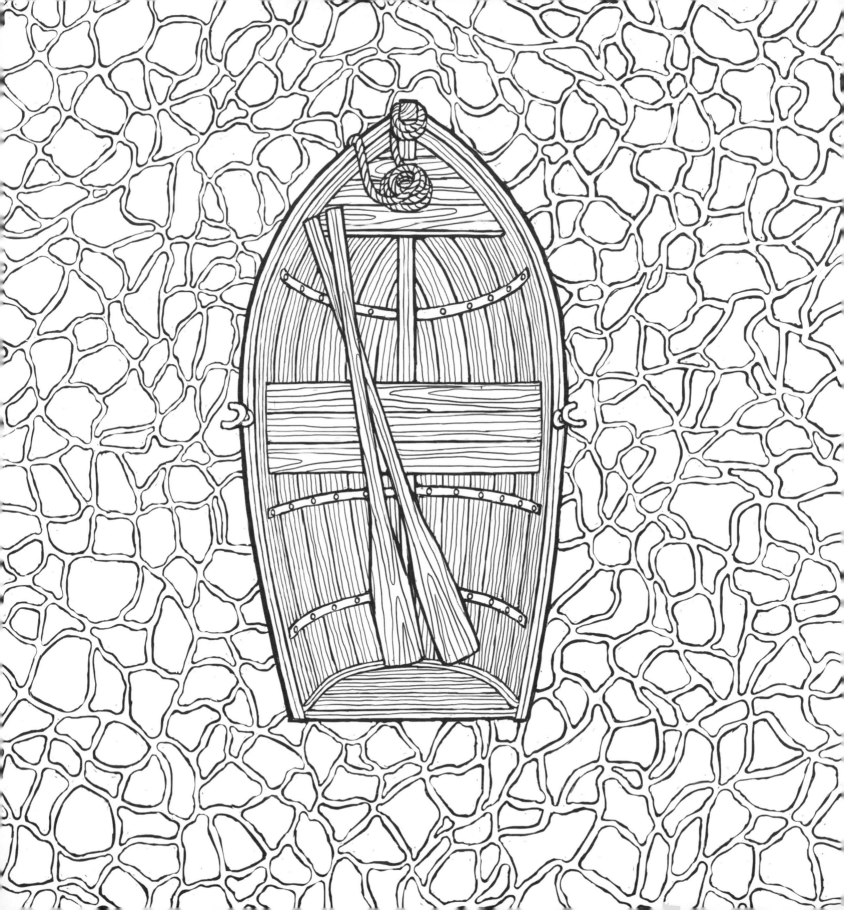

"A grandfather tells his grandson,
'Two wolves are fighting in my heart. One wolf is angry,
fearful, envious, resentful, deceitful. The other wolf is
kind, compassionate, honest, generous, and wise.'
The grandson asks which wolf will win the fight.
The grandfather answers,
'The one I feed.'"

CHEROKEE PARABLE

"To live is so startling it leaves little time
for anything else."

EMILY DICKINSON
AMERICAN POET

(1830–1886)

"Rivers know this: there is no hurry.
We shall get there some day."

A.A. MILNE
ENGLISH AUTHOR AND POET
(1882–1956)

MEDITATION ON COLORING

Find a comfortable, well-supported spot to sit and arrange everything you need—your pens or pencils and your sharpener.

Before you start, take a moment to locate yourself in your body. Close your eyes and become aware of your feet on the floor, feel how your seat supports you. Notice if there is any tension and try to let it go. Pay attention to how your breath rises and falls.

Now open you eyes and choose an image. Notice what happens when you look at the picture. Does it conjure up thoughts, memories or feelings? Note the state of your mind. Is it calm or ruffled?

Select your colors and take a pencil or pen in your hand. How does it feel? Are you holding it firmly or loosely? We don't have to be slow to be mindful, but slowing things down can help to remind us to pay attention. There is no rush to complete the picture. As you color, notice how much pressure you apply to the paper, how many strokes it takes to fill each space, how the colors interact with one another and how the whole picture is gradually coming to life.

Also try to maintain a general awareness of the body and breath as you work. This can help you to feel grounded in the activity. When you notice that your thoughts have wandered, just gently return to your breath and the activity.

REFLECTIONS

The texts and images in this section have explored the theme of mindfulness. Take a moment now to think about how working on them has helped you develop your own practice. How easy has it been to recognize the quality when it arises? Many people find that when they start practicing mindfulness it seems as though their mind is more chaotic than ever. This is because they are becoming more aware of the way their mind works. The following questions and ideas will help you reflect on your own experience.

REVIEWING YOUR WORK

Ask yourself the following questions—you may want to note your answers down on a piece of paper:

- How did you feel as you began coloring? And as you finished?
- When did you find it easy to maintain mindfulness? When was it hard?
- Can you recall where you felt particularly aware or calm, and can you pinpoint this moment on the page?
- What have you learnt from trying to be more mindful?

EXPLORING MINDFULNESS IN YOUR DAILY LIFE

Think of some other times of the day when you can make a point of practicing mindfulness. For example, when you're chopping vegetables, washing the dishes, walking to and from work, or eating your meals.

How do you find this? Is it easier to maintain mindfulness during some activities rather than others?

Thich Nhat Hanh, a Zen master and author of many books on mindfulness talks about "bells of mindfulness." These are seemingly mundane events that happen regularly in our lives that we can transform into reminders, or "alarm bells" to be present. For example: a red traffic light, flicking a light switch, a neighbor's barking dog. Find a bell of mindfulness in your life.

The next time you have a conversation with a friend or colleague, make a point of bringing your attention fully to what they are saying. Consider if this changes the way you listen.

Children are naturally mindful. See if you can spend some time with a child (your own or someone else's), really immersing yourself in their world. Let them teach you how to stay in the moment.

IN YOUR JOURNAL

Start to make a regular journal entry to chart your practice. You might want to include times when you have been coloring, or other times in the day when you have tried to be more mindful. Make a note of how it went and any ideas you have that will help you develop your practice.

NOTES ... DOODLES ... IDEAS ... SCRIBBLES ... THOUGHTS ...

INSIGHT

When we *really* look at something, and stay present with it, we begin to understand it and it can teach us not just about itself, but also about the whole world.

The teachings in this section are an eclectic mix. At first sight it might seem as though there is little connecting them: they discuss subject matters as diverse as friendship, nature, fresh perspectives, and happiness. But, despite the apparent diversity, we felt they were united in the way they evoke wonder; some recognize it in the details, and others "nudge" us towards seeing that wonder by pointing out our capacity to experience it.

Each speaker recognizes something profound and wonderful about the world, and the eyes that perceive it, and so helps us to see that truth too.

"When one door closes, another door opens; but we so often look so long and so regretfully upon the closed door that we do not see the ones that open for us."

ALEXANDER GRAHAM BELL
SCOTTISH INVENTOR

(1847–1922)

"There is a candle in your heart, ready to be kindled.
There is a void in your soul, ready to be filled.
You feel it, don't you?"

RUMI
SUFI POET AND PHILOSOPHER

(1207–1273)

"A single sunbeam is enough to drive away many shadows."

ST. FRANCIS OF ASSISI
ITALIAN CATHOLIC PREACHER

(c. 1181–1226)

"Every blade in the field—every leaf in the forest—
lays down its life in its season as beautifully
as it was taken up."

HENRY DAVID THOREAU
AMERICAN WRITER AND PHILOSOPHER

(1817–1862)

"The temple bell stops—
but the sound keeps coming
out of the flowers."

MATSUO BASHO
JAPANESE HAIKU MASTER

(1644–1694)

"Friendship is a sheltering tree."

SAMUEL TAYLOR COLERIDGE
ENGLISH POET

(1772–1834)

"For in the dew of little things the heart finds its morning and is refreshed."

KHALIL GIBRAN
LEBANESE-AMERICAN POET AND ARTIST

(1883–1931)

"The clearest way into the Universe
is through a forest wilderness."

JOHN MUIR
SCOTTISH-BORN AMERICAN NATURALIST AND WRITER

(1838–1914)

"The real voyage of discovery consists not in seeking
new landscapes but in having new eyes."

MARCEL PROUST
FRENCH NOVELIST AND CRITIC

(1871–1922)

"The mind, once stretched by a new idea,
never returns to its original dimensions."

RALPH WALDO EMERSON
AMERICAN ESSAYIST, LECTURER AND POET

(1803–1882)

MEDITATION ON A PENCIL

Find a comfortable, well-supported spot to sit.

Before you start, take a moment to locate yourself in your body. Close your eyes and become aware of your feet on the floor, feel how your seat supports you. Notice if there is any tension and try to let it go. Pay attention to how your breath rises and falls.

Now open your eyes and take a colored pencil in your hand. Turn it over. Notice the wood. Smell it. Is it freshly sharpened, or discolored from use?

Bring to mind the tree that provided this wood. Bring to mind the sun that warmed its leaves, the rain that watered it and the soil that nourished it. Imagine the breeze ruffling its leaves. Consider the creatures that made their home in this tree.

Call to mind the workers who felled the tree and raised it onto a truck for transportation. Imagine its journey to the sawmill. Hear the saws and machines that cut the wood and shaped it.

Bring to mind the factory that produced this pencil. Feel the heat of the fire that boiled the pigment, and the machine that extruded the pencil lead. Call to mind the machines that shaped the wood, glued it, and sharpened the pencil. Consider the workers who inspected it.

Bring to mind the journey of the pencil to a store, and then its journey to your hand.

Consider what marks are inside this pencil, ready to be freed onto the page.

REFLECTIONS

Working on the drawings in this section encourages us to find insight. Looking closely at the world with a non-judgemental mind increases our sense of wonder.

Take a moment now to consider how these texts and images have resonated with you. The following questions and ideas will help you to review your insights and think about how you can make use of these in your own world.

REVIEWING YOUR WORK

Grab a piece of paper and a pen and ponder the following questions:

- What did you enjoy coloring most? Why?
- Consider how you relate to the images before you color them, while coloring, and once you have finished. When do you look most closely at them?
- Can you think where the text has given you a fresh perspective on the image, or where the image has enabled a deeper understanding of the text?
- Is there a link between your level of awareness and your ability to appreciate beauty?

DISCOVERING INSIGHT IN YOUR DAILY LIFE

Go into the garden or the local park and spend a few minutes looking very closely at a small area of nature. Try to let any judgements slip away, as you focus entirely on what you see. Make a note of what arises.

Consider what sights fill you with awe and make a special plan to observe them. It could be a natural phenomenon, such as the night sky or a waterfall, or it could be man-made, such as a painting, a suspension bridge, or a wind farm.

Collect together a list of things in your life that fill you with wonder and gratitude. This could be family, the sunshine, a favorite tree, the taste of orange juice—or anything that makes you happy. Try representing these elements of your life with pictures and then put them together to create a "vision board." You can display this somewhere in your home.

Think about areas of your life that are challenging, and consider whether you hold beliefs that are limiting you. Try to look at the situation without judgment. To help you do that you might want to experiment with alternative viewpoints. For example a belief such as "I'm no good with money" can be transformed into "I have an opportunity to learn how to manage my money better."

IN YOUR JOURNAL

Find something that fills you with wonder each day. Make a note of it and of how it makes you feel. Try drawing it. Can you think of any words that could accompany the picture?

NOTES ... DOODLES ... IDEAS ... SCRIBBLES ... THOUGHTS ...

INSPIRATION

We found the quotations in this section to be particularly valuable in reminding us how much influence our actions have on the world, and how we need to take responsibility for ourselves.

The speakers and writers we have included come from a diverse range of backgrounds. However, each recognizes the transformative power of good thoughts and deeds. Some speak of the courage we need to take positive action—whether that's within ourselves or in the wider community. Others draw attention to the fact that each skilful action or thought, no matter how small, can serve as a beacon of light in the darkness.

We hope that these teachings and images empower you too, and help you to see the wider value of your inner journey.

"Don't look for big things,
just do small things with great love."

MOTHER TERESA
ALBANIAN MISSIONARY

(1910–1997)

"What you do makes a difference, and you have to decide what kind of difference you want to make."

DAME JANE GOODALL
ENGLISH PRIMATOLOGIST AND ETHOLOGIST
(B. 1934)

"When watching after yourself, you watch after others.
When watching after others, you watch after yourself."

GAUTAMA BUDDHA
INDIAN SPIRITUAL LEADER

(c. 600–300 BCE)

"Be kind whenever possible. It is always possible."

HIS HOLINESS THE 14TH DALAI LAMA

(B. 1935)

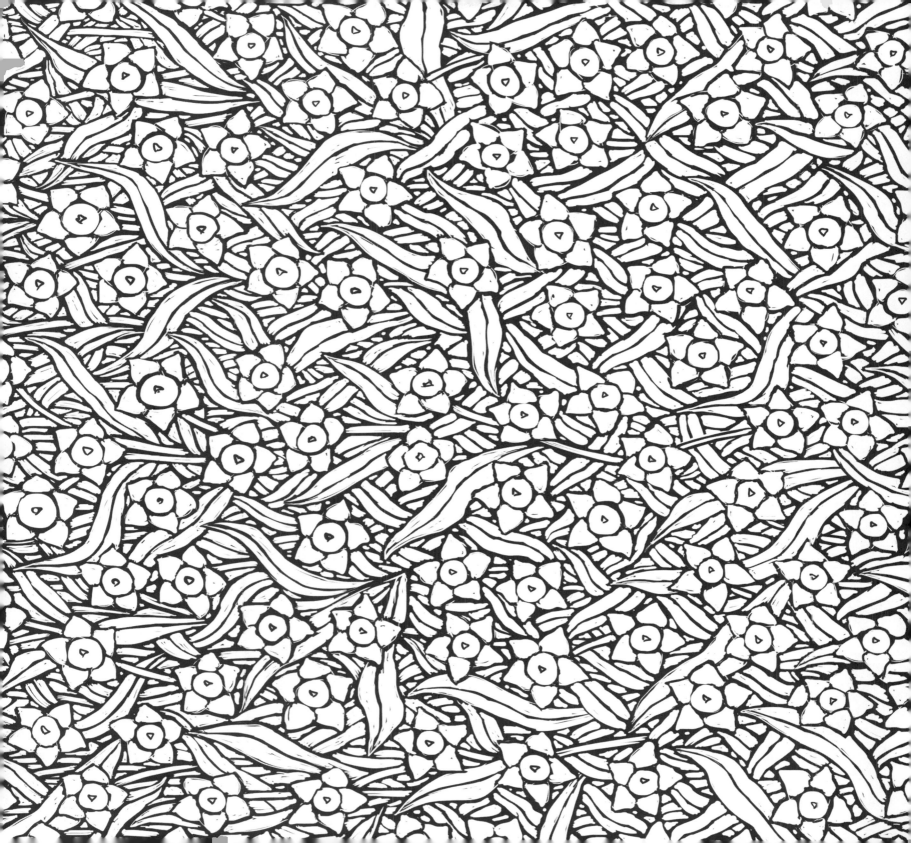

"So never lose an opportunity of urging a practical beginning, however small, for it is wonderful how often in such matters the mustard seed germinates and roots itself."

FLORENCE NIGHTINGALE
ENGLISH NURSE AND SOCIAL REFORMER

(1820–1910)

"The man who moves a mountain
begins by carrying away small stones."

CONFUCIUS
CHINESE PHILOSOPHER

(551–479 BCE)

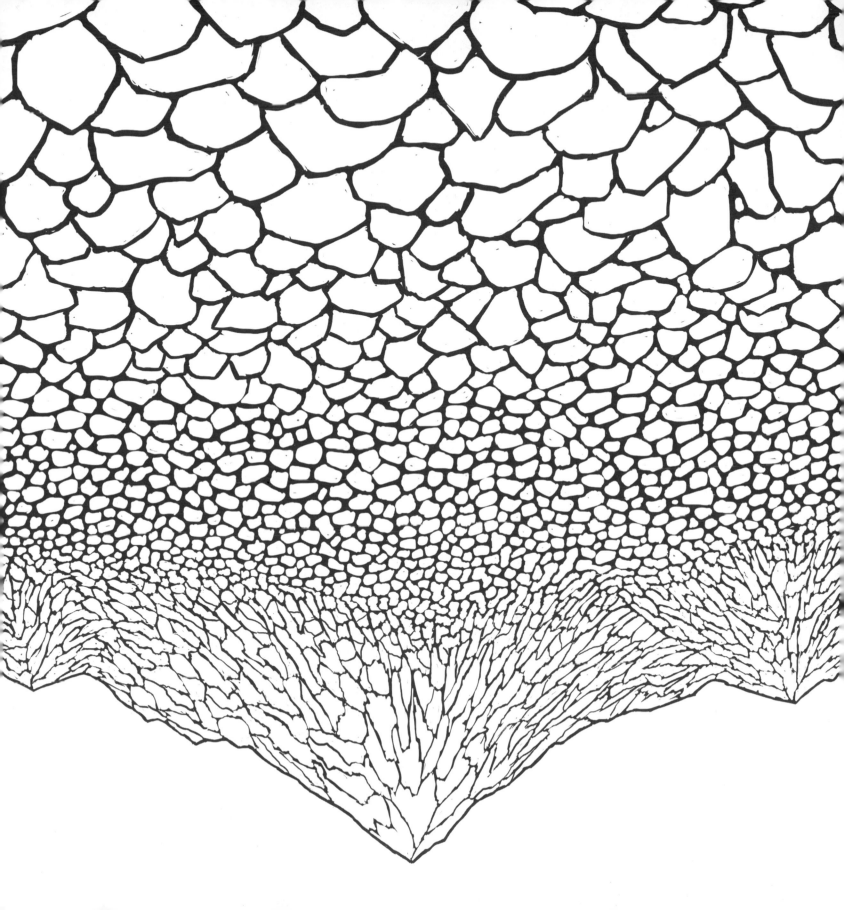

"A human being is a part of a whole, called by us 'Universe,' a part limited in time and space. He experiences himself, his thoughts and feelings as something separated from the rest—a kind of optical delusion of his consciousness. This delusion is a kind of prison for us, restricting us to our personal desires and to affection for a few persons nearest to us. Our task must be to free ourselves from this prison by widening our circles of compassion to embrace all living creatures and the whole of nature in its beauty."

ALBERT EINSTEIN
GERMAN PHYSICIST

(1879–1955)

"True love is boundless like the ocean and,
swelling within one, spreads itself out and,
crossing all boundaries and frontiers,
envelops the whole world."

MAHATMA GANDHI
INDIAN ACTIVIST AND INDEPENDENCE LEADER

(1869–1948)

"Forget conventionalisms; forget what the
world thinks of you stepping out of your place;
think your best thoughts, speak your best words,
work your best works, looking to your own
conscience for approval."

SUSAN B. ANTHONY
AMERICAN CIVIL RIGHTS LEADER

(1820–1906)

"How wonderful it is that nobody need wait a single moment before starting to improve the world."

ANNE FRANK
GERMAN JEWISH DIARIST

(1929–1945)

MEDITATION ON LOVING-KINDNESS

The following meditation is adapted from traditional Buddhist teaching, which says that the cultivation of loving-kindness, or *metta*, towards both yourself and all others is a path to happiness and liberation.

Find a comfortable, well-supported spot to sit.

Before you start, take a moment to locate yourself in your body. Close your eyes and become aware of your feet on the floor, feel how your seat supports you. Notice if there is any tension and try to let it go. Pay attention to how your breath rises and falls.

Silently repeat the following phrase: "May I be well and happy," while sending these wishes towards yourself. If you prefer, you can change the words to something that resonates more deeply with you. For example, "May I be at ease," "May I be content," "May I let go of trouble and stress."

As you speak see if you can call up a feeling of wellbeing towards yourself. Don't worry if you can't, just keep repeating the phrase.

When you are ready, send these wishes outwards, towards all other beings, now saying, "May they be well and happy." Spend a few moments repeating the phrase. Try to include everybody, without exclusion. You might like to bring to mind specific people to help you open up these good wishes. Start with someone who has helped you, then a friend, someone you feel neutral towards, and finally someone you find challenging. Even if it is difficult, try to wish them the same good wishes you have wished for yourself.

REFLECTIONS

The drawings in this section have focused on inspiration and, in particular, how we can transform our own sense of balance and connectedness into a force for good in the world. Use this opportunity now to consider how you have been inspired by these texts and images, or perhaps by other events or conversations you have had recently.

REVIEWING YOUR WORK

Take a few moments to consider the following questions:

- Which pictures or texts particularly resonated with you? Were any of them particularly inspiring?
- Can you think of any areas in your life that could benefit from these ideas?
- When you did the meditation, did you find it harder to direct loving-kindness towards some people than others? If so, why?
- Can you think of a sentence or two that sums up your own life philosophy?
- What kind of picture would you draw to represent that?

ACTING ON INSPIRATION IN YOUR DAILY LIFE

Think of specific small activities you could do each day to show loving-kindness towards yourself, such as listening to a favorite piece of music or indulging in a long soak in the bath. Every now and then, you can do some bigger things too, such as treating yourself to a new outfit, or going for a special night out. When you wish yourself more loving-kindness, you have more resources to give out to others, too.

Walk around your house and fill up a box of things that you don't need any more, but that others could use. Give them away to friends or a charity thrift store. Notice how you feel as you practice generosity.

As you go through your day, try to spread more goodwill wherever you can. This could be as simple as holding the door open for somebody, giving way to another car, or signing a petition. Try to make every action you do a positive one.

When opportunities arise to help others in bigger ways, try to be open to them. This might be signing up for a charity run or perhaps making a commitment to shop more ethically.

IN YOUR JOURNAL

Start taking notice of when you receive loving-kindness from others and when you feel loving-kindness towards them. Be aware of times when you could express more loving-kindness, either through feeling or action.

NOTES ... DOODLES ... IDEAS ... SCRIBBLES ... THOUGHTS ...

THE FOLLOWING QUOTES ARE REPRODUCED WITH KIND PERMISSION.

Page 28 Reprinted from *The Long Road Turns to Joy: A Guide to Walking Meditation* (1996) by Thich Nhat Hanh, with permission of Parallax Press, Berkeley, California, www.parallax.org

Page 38 From *Pooh's Little Instruction Book*, inspired by A. A. Milne, © 1995 by the Trustees of the Pooh Properties, original text and compilation of illustrations. Used by permission of Dutton Children's Books, an imprint of Penguin Young Readers Group, a division of Penguin Random House LLC.

Page 72 *The Writings of Mother Teresa of Calcutta* © by the Mother Teresa Center, exclusive licensee throughout the world of the Missionaries of Charity for the works of Mother Teresa

Page 74 © Dr Jane Goodall DBE, Founder of the Jane Goodall Institute and UN Messenger of Peace, www.janegoodall.org.uk, www.janegoodall.org, www.rootsnshoots.org.uk

Page 78 Reprinted with permission from the office of His Holiness the 14th Dalai Lama

Page 85 Albert Einstein to Norman Salit, March 14, 1950, on the occasion of the death of Salit's daughter. AEA 61-226. © The Hebrew University of Jerusalem

Page 90 © Anne Frank Fonds, Basel, Switzerland